Fleeting Feelings

Surya D. Adhikarla

Contents

Living with Myself

Passion

I want to be so close to you that I can peep in
your imagination; going beyond my own
and find that you feel the same thing
in the same way and feel myself at home

Departing to a place just you and me
alone; scared by the thought but the heart craves
a strange loneliness keeps stalking us,
our desire is the only thing that stays and saves

Not a moment that we leave the other's
side; not a moment to be left waste
Not a moment there is that feels dry,
We fill our thirst drinking from the other's eye

Settling their accounts paying the debt for separation,
Destroying the division with this fatal attraction,
Our bodies cling to one another with such determination,
Even a thought finds no way to enter this amalgamation

Two souls combine into one as we hug,
each other; with my arms I surround you,
smothered in the passion as we come close,
As if stuck by something stronger than glue

There will no more be you and me,
When we come close, it's going to be
Only one feeling, one body as long as we breathe,
Lost in one another for an entire eternity!

I dance!

Nothing's going to stop me tonight,
I'm excited and going on a wild ride,

This is the time I forget myself
Immersed in this feeling of senselessness

The music from the stereo is filled in me
Every beat coming out is guiding me

I groove, I move, I stoop & I get up
I shriek, I shout, I cry & I shut up

Everything starts to blur in the euphoria of dance
I lay hands everywhere as if there isn't another chance

Now that I lost control, I'm in charge of the floor,
I move around so much that I feel the motion no more,

A desire not to stop even for a second takes over,
I tremble, I falter but still I hold the beat and recover,

When I roll everyone should stand still to see me
And when I stop & look, they all should feel dizzy

I ain't no pro but I can mix well with the beat
Make you motionless with the movement of my feet

This is my dance and it makes me feel complete
And I will never stop doing it until I cease to exist

B-Alive

I could hear spades and shovels,
I felt the floating one was me,
I could hear voices around whispering,
I thought it was a dream.

Within no time I fell in a pit,
Laid in a box covered with a lid,
If only I spoke they would've know I didn't die,
Now I get what happened, I was buried alive.

At first I panicked and I tried to shout,
Then just settled to making some noise,
When I felt that something was moving,
Whenever I heard some voice.

I kept turning in my grave,
Think ng how I ended in this nightmare,
Sealed in the stupid coffin,
Counting my breaths in stale air.

I feel a creeping sensation up my spine,
Though I know it's the feeling of disgust
At 6 feet deep under normal life,
But I console myself saying it's the dust.

I could sense seeds sprouting at my feet,
worms crawling up to find something to eat,
Every cell in my body starts to dry, I fall asleep,
Slowly degenerating and mixing with the weeds.

But after I lose the last ray of light,
I will let my soul haunt this place with unending cries,
To silence the dead and alert the living,
And make sure no one is again buried alive!

Nightmare

A silent cool breeze under the moonlight,
seems like an invite to a snake fight,
in a calm and bizarre village night,
where the path is safe as long as it's in sight.

The rogue zephyr wheedling the leaves,
lulling all the senses and making them fall asleep,
or putting them in a trance in order to deceive,
like a traitor ready to burn the land on which he sleeps.

My heart keeps warning me not to believe,
no matter how intimate it may appear to be,
more intense in the form of fear it is,
causing things unknown that I can't even see.

Stranded in strange village with an eerie vicinity,
left to face an invisible foe; an eccentric calamity,
a hexed imagination I am left to wander in free,
asphyxiated by the smoke of my burning dreams!

GMJ RIP

" It was no mistake of mine! "
His last words made me lose my mind
They pierced my heart and tore it apart
Like taking a wet paper and pressing it hard
An innocent he was, ignorant of world's ways
He sure was someone who deserved a better place
But what happened doesn't see fair at all
He had to pay the price though it wasn't his fault
What he said hangs like a question in the air
No one has an answer to it and no one does dare
The pyre burns, smoke raises as we stare
At the loss of another soul for something that seems
unfair!!

How! can I see thou?

Look into my eyes, they're sunk deep inside,
how do you expect them to look at you and smile!
Day in & day out they stare at the LCD,
d(r)ying in search of something; to do is to be
The eyes which once held a bundle of dreams,
had to let them roll away in silent streams!
The ones which used to express out happiness,
now indicate dizziness & seem directionless.
Those that cried at the time of separation from friends,
are now tired of looking them at a distance.
Those that had a habit of counting sheep,
row look dried up deprived of sleep.
Look into these eyes and notice the difference,
a look from them might seem a stare but they mean no
offense.
How can I look at your beauty with eyes like these,
If they fail to recognize you, excuse them please.

I am Water

There is a continuous flow of thoughts in my brain,
like the water that flows from terrain to terrain.
as the path for the water is made by rocks and blocks,
my perceptions & the situations shape my thoughts,
occasionally, as the water stands still,
I am caught by some thought against my will,
but the state is ephemeral till there is a way out,
momentum is regained and I move further
I am water.

I am Fire

I got a trier in me,
I got a hell lot of desire in me,
A passion that can burn anything in vicinity,
A hunger to know and keep glowing till eternity,
Burning myself, molding at every chance,
Heading to my goal aggressive as a lance,
Face any situation, no matter how dire,
I am fire

Disappointed

It's almost dark outside,
Dusk has fallen but the light is bright
Sitting at the desk I write

I am feeling empty, I don't know why,
Is it because there is no one around me or
That I am not occupied

Your smile is a beautiful lie,
Lyrics of "Stereo love" haunting my mind,
My head seems to have empty chambers inside

A letter addressed to me,
From a friend who wants to advise
That I don't know the value of what I have

A silent wish not to cry,
To call you and tell the reason why,
I could not make it that day and let you fly.

Bearing the pain all the time,
Of the ring you put on my finger that night,
Can't remove it as it reminds me of the times we had

Broken promises, dreams and lies,
Unspoken desires, feelings that I deny,
Losing hope with every sigh, leading an incomplete life!

I wish I were

I wish I were a machine
Cleared of feeling; 'clean'
Beyond the scope and scene
Of heartly things unseen

I'd have no reason to hate
To blame, to cry on my fate
To like or love for no reason
No departs', no need to have pain

Predefining my work what's what
Doing without any second thought
Completing everything completely
Ain't wasting time in affairs dreamily

I wish I were a machine
Then maybe I'd be left unseen
If I were a machine of course
I'd not have written this in remorse

Ambivalence

Endless silence shouting at me
That I'm discarding its company

Thinking of someone far apart
Who left her prints in my heart

Counting on her images that I see
Don't know how or where is she

Clinging to an unseen rope
The other end is tight I just hope

Mind rejects to admit her absence
Now I'm wincing here in reminiscence

Struggling hard in space and time
Feel like a second persists for a lifetime

Mix with the silence! What else can I do?
Let me find a way out, I have no choice but to

Wait till my next life or find someone new
To feel the old joy or start this state anew!

Rain

It started raining now,
Everything will get wet somehow
I stand near the glass window
Wondering if only I can go

Out there, in the rain and get wet
Feel the cool water fall on my head
I would jump in the water that lies on the ground
and create a big tide for the ants coming along

I would run along the street
Without my shoes, on bare feet
I'd sprinkle water at places
where I see any dry spaces

After the rain stops, I'd catch the nearest plant
Shake it thorough, letting water drop from each branch
coz mom will dry my hair so that I won't catch cold
but I haven't seen anyone do the same with it, poor soul

The rain is stopping, it's work here is done,
but I am still inside, I don't know when it will return
I simply stare standing near the glass window
Wishing one day, out there, I will go

Can I apologize?

I was happy I wasn't sad,
I guess I dint realize that I was mad,
a new person beside me was all that I had
I should have known I was a meandering lad

I stepped into a territory unknown,
told myself it's a common feeling, I am not alone,
I listened to what they said and was completely blown,
I said I love you, I made you cry and now I moan

I am sorry to have disturbed your world,
I never thought I couldn't even be bold,
to carry out with the relation as I told,
now I feel like a spoiled doll hung to be sold

I wonder/awe at what maturity can do,
proves it false that once we thought was true,
it's hard to digest what I have done to you,
I realize I bit more than I can chew

I feel helpless, I get nothing to my mind,
I can't bring back the past but if only things could rewind,
I wouldn't ,in the first place, let our paths intertwine,
I would have saved you from the selfish acts of mine.

now on, it's a small curse I carry with every sunrise,
every pair I see brings tears in my eyes,
if you can, please forget me and lead a happy life,
it's been a terrible mistake on my part, can I apologize?

A place

There's a place far away from this door,
a place where sometimes I wish to go!
where the bed is warm and the music is slow,
where I am myself, a place called home.

Where life is at peace and hours move like days,
I chat with the wood burning in the fire place.
listening to LOG stories and watching the smoke trace,
serenity dawns on me carving a smile on my face.

Slipping thoughts

Poems of the night never see the day
Inebriated thoughts cannot seem to stay
They wander in the dark alone
Abandoned, with a mind of their own
Preaching some practical truth
That's laughed at for lack of proof
Orphaned thoughts born out of care
Emotions & feeling hidden unaware
Poems of the night never see the day
Hard to recognize (them) under a sober stare

Fleeting Feelings

Let me tell you a story about a girl and a guy
don't ask when it happened, how did it and why
picture these fellas in the middle of a stream downhill
one on each rock separated by the flow they stood still
neither was worried, they knew their ships were coming
along
but deep in their heart they were sacred, something was
going wrong
it was the look that each got from the other
both were equally enticed by the glance of the other
as if they were forced by something unseen
unseen but something they felt deep within
part attraction and part desire
that stirred in their heart a chilling fire
an urge to dive and cross the stream
if only they could move, it was all like a dream
they weren't aware how to swim, their hearts moaned
though the boy seemed to have a strong will & the girl- a
weak wont
caught between helplessness and desperation it was
hard to breathe
they wore a mask of serenity but were suffocating
beneath
it dint last long, the girl was ready to go, her ship was
coming near
realizing the reality, the heart started to shed its fear
the water seemed to slow down, time seemed to blow off
the fire
all the feelings seemed to disappear, there was no more
desire
how fleeting the mind is, though for a moment it holds
you in tight grip
u feel it so real, when it goes it leaves a regretting twitch
on the lip
thus parts the boy from the girl, the girl from the guy,
don't ask me how should you interpret it, what I wish to
say and why !

Daunting Dusk

A stench of stillness
and temptation of rain
A dreadful dullness
with persistence of stain

Reminiscent of the pain
From belligerent regret
Insinuating an arcane
And sardonic sunset

With a warrior's expertise
Clear and surprisingly quiet
Inducing immense unease
Seemingly unarmed twilight

Visit

When the sun drops down the horizon,
when the darkness starts to spread on,
as I am done with my chores,
I hear her knocking on my doors.

she comes to me at night, in my favorite attire,
rushes in and shuts the door behind her tight.
she says we don't have much time together,
this is all that we have and pulls me near.

never minding the time, we roam around places.
as I lay on her lap, she caresses my face.
I share my thoughts my wishes and my dreams.
she listens intently to everything I say.

sensing the arrival of dawn, she stops me in my tracks.
as if to answer the disappointment in my eyes,
asking me to keep this visit a secret rite,
she promises to return the next night.

That place, that state

The deserted streets with neon lights
That didn't show any sign of life

Dragging myself to that room
Something I labeled as my home

Trying the best to keep my spirits up
Not to lose hope in such morose setup

A phase of my life I can never forget
For I held myself tight so as not to regret

That emptiness knew no bounds
The nothingness made me astound

How I got stuck in such a place
Couldn't breathe even when it was desolate

Desperately holding on to that light
Just like to the street lamp burning post-midnight

I held myself together with a reason
To see the sunrise shining on an Eden

Where I would go far from these things
consoling myself that I am paying off for my sins

Wishing myself goodnight

On your delicate feet silently my way,
Walk upon the clouds to descend now
And silently seep into my eyes

From the Kingdom of moon far away
Guided by the angles and their songs
Glide o! Sleep into my eyes

The little glowing lights
Mysterious fireflies
Become one with the Stars

And begin whispering
As the eyes start closing
sweet lullaby of some sorts

Dream away my dear
Receive what you deserve
Drift into the magical lands

As the night falls near
Reenergize your vigor
Resting your head on your hands

An island far away

I have set up a small life on this island
I don't remember how I drifted in my plan
Sailing on the ocean towards the west
And Reached to this nearest dry land

Engulfed in darkness for most of the day
I cover myself in a blanket and lay
Afraid of being awake for a long time
Alone in a place I have created to stay

When my body gets tired of lying asleep
I go out to get something to eat
Spotting an occasional fruit or some root
I bring enough for a day from the woods deep

The sun comes up early and so does the night
As if even the sky here keeps its eyes shut tight
For it stays dark till an eternity, before I go back
into my cave as I spot the arrival of the first light

I have created a habit to retain my sanity
Besides keeping myself alive, the routine I keep
I found some broken logs beside the stream
using which I was able to create some heat

I sit with my face towards the raising fire
Like a child it asks for a story jumping higher
I open a blank page in the book of my mind
To jot down my imaginations till I retire

Looking to the sky, at the star in the east
I start to imagine the lives piece by piece
Of each person with the face of my friend
Recollecting my home that lies overseas

Coming to terms with parents of her beloved
I imagine the girl I knew smile and shout
As their match is fixed after all the trouble
excitement in her life screaming the most loud

I imagine a grand wedding of a friend
A celebration resembling that in heaven
Amidst his family and all his relatives
And the cheers of all peers who attend

Conveying the news of her newborn on phone
A baby boy; Of the lady that I have known
I imagine her thinking of her spouse
Who is trying his best to be back home

And so, on I let the horse of my imagination
Gallop and run wild to its satisfaction
And let it trot back when it is tired
I will tie it in the stable of this strange fiction

But Sometimes I think of all this and feel
What if someone comes here and finds me
Or if I somehow travel back to my land
& listen to their story- which one would I believe

Until then I will keep imagining their lives
considering myself in touch in my own style
Probably my story would trump their reality
And they like their lives in the way I see

It was Love

Dressed in a very casual attire
I start walking towards the place
It is evening and slightly raining
Streets are silent, I do not see a face

I know I am going to a graveyard
But cannot recollect for whom
Whose funeral am I attending
I feel it is someone I knew

I see vermillion hues in the sky and
Rain trying to clear them for the night
I hear my footsteps echoing with splashes
Urging me to hurry up for the rite

I finally reach and stand at a grave
but no one seems to arrive
somehow, I know this is the right one
It's just me, I feel pity for the dead guy

To have no one come to his funeral
he must be alone or have turned lonely
But then I wonder at my presence
Is this someone close to me?

I feel anxious with guilt and shame
For not remembering who it is
I notice the feeling is a bit different
I get scared I don't hear my heart beat

I move close and sit down trying to read
What's written on the stone in front of me
I am taken aback, a part of me understands
but I try hard to deny what it really means

I wake up with a disappointing sense of unease
My mind starts going over the entire scene
A resigned feeling and an ache in my chest tell me
That it was the love in me that died in the dream

Last thing on my mind

The shining stars reflect in the glass
full of wine,
I sit in the corner looking at the moon
in the sky,
There is so much stress,
There is loneliness,
but the last thing on my mind is regret.

Memories of the past come back
and remind,
the feelings I conveyed to you
that night,
for all the things said,
for everything I felt,
the last thing on my mind is regret.

All these thoughts make me lose
track of time,
empty bottles fall from the table
making noise,
there goes from sight,
another sleepless night,
but the last thing on my mind is regret

Dreaming of Demons

Under the moon-lit night and their venoms
Windless and silent, never ending and violent
Smug and dry, something close to a bad memory
No matter how much I fight no end I foresee

They keep on pounding, astounding their number is
I keep rebounding and grounding them on their knees
Relentless and angry pointlessly targeting me
Seeking some forgotten revenge that I did not agree

Slaying them at a speed exceeding their reach
Losing myself to the chore, neither happy nor angry
My actions mechanical as if a long pending responsibility
Observing and observant at the same instant, I dream

Confusing and contriving a crisis beyond my belief
Incomprehensible my subconscious's message to me
Concluding that I can never decipher what I see
I roll over my bed instead of stopping it in between

One more time

(ode to my four years of engineering)
One more time I want to walk through that gate,
One more time want to be 5 minutes late,
One more time want to run for the class,
One more time want to get scolded for coming last.

One more time I want to sit beside my friend,
near the wall , in that row, at this end,
One more time I want to sleep during the class
One more time want to be caught by Mr.Das

One more time I want to dance on that stage,
One more time want my friends to clap with full rage,
One more time want to stay till the beats cease
One more time want to hear - Once more please

One more time want to live those 4 years,
One more time want you all to be my peers,
One more time want to smile before I cry,
One more time want to be with you or just die

p.s. *Mr.P.K.Das our prof.*

Love and Loss

Walking away

She is walking away,
Unaware of my feelings, unaware of my thoughts,
Unaware that my heart today is falling apart!

She is walking away,
Stepping on my memories, crushing them like dried
leaves,
Leaving me behind in my boulevard of broken dreams.

She is walking away,
With heart full of hopes, and a gleeful smile on the face,
Head high in the air, distancing herself with every step
she takes.

She is walking away,
To be another person, to make her life complete,
To another world of her own, to join a different league.

She is walking away,
With great achievement to join the celebration of a life
time,
Leaving her imprints on a statue made in the shape of
mine.

She is walking away,
And I stand still, stranded and lost in the void,
Happy to see her enjoy, though a part of me is
destroyed.

Blue Light

When sun has finally set for the day
When all the birds have flown away
She returns to the home tired and grey
Gets refreshed, takes food and prays

She comes to me and says,
Switch on the blue light
Come and sit close to me
Take my hand and hold it tight
I want to sleep

I want to put everything else beside
Just you, me and this blue light
A magical moment that eases my mind
I relax on your shoulder, a bliss divine

She sits close to me hugging at my waist
Puts her head on my shoulder, silently we gaze
Into the sea through the window hearing the waves
While I move the swing we are on, at slow pace

Just before she is swallowed by her sleep she says,
Please keep on the blue light
I will sleep hearing the sea
I may get a nightmare tonight
I want you to tightly hug me

She slips slowly into sleep
And appears to be so calm and at ease
She appears breathtaking; the breeze
takes away her stress and sings a lullaby sweet

as my eyes turn moist, I go and switch off the blue light
It's been a long time, she now rests in peace
And I can't spend another sleepless night
In her memories etched in my heart so deep

Lovers

In the scorching heat and the deserted place,
I see an upset expression on that beautiful face.
The tour was supposed to be fun and a thrilling one,
But her dry smile depicts an intended pun.

She looks at her boyfriend, who brings the lemonade,
Tired from all the roaming they rejuvenate in the shade.
Though sweat keeps piling on my eyebrows I do not fail
to notice,
The subtle expressions they exchange which no one
else sees.
It fills my heart with a warm feeling and I wonder how
simple it is,
To communicate with the other if there is love and you
are at ease.

I look at them with great interest till the point that I don't
blink,
Slowly I stop wondering and my mind starts to think.
What question is being asked and what answer is being
given,
What apprehension is she showing, what assurance is
he giving!

The state of being in love so naïve yet so esoteric,
Realized when mature yet it makes people act
sophomoric.
It elates you and brings you one step closer to divinity,
By equipping your senses with additional capability.
You talk with your sight, you think with your heart,
You exist as a whole but be someone else's part.

As I lose the sense of reality theorizing the scene in front
of me,
The whistle from the ship pinches and pulls me back to
the sea.
The mood is set and we start for the next coast in the
list,
Holding my thoughts I follow them quick, to experience
second hand bliss.

I look at you and I couldn't breathe
You looked at me and my heart skipped a beat
I realized what 'mesmerized' meant
Before I knew it, my heart developed feet

It was just a while ago that you left my side
Not so long apart, to say a day and a night
But somehow, I lost the sense of time
Felt like I am seeing you after a pretty long flight

The moth gets pulled towards the burning light,
Unaware of the consequence, unaware of what it is like,
Believe me or not, you attract me like a moth,
You are my source of energy, you r my killing strike

There's an excitement when you look at me
An enthusiasm that you can't see,
restlessness starts piling in my heart,
when you are nowhere in the vicinity!

Every day with you is worth a thousand years
you are my purpose you are my drive
I shine in your love, i glow with each moment
you are the only reason to keep me alive

loneliness burns me to ashes every night
it's difficult to be without you by my side
it's really hard and I don't deny but like a phoenix
I am born again in the morning with your sight

A promise

When we came we knew none,
started interacting one by one,
had some quarrels, had some fun,
but still it seems something's undone.

freshers, youth force, blood camp, SEEE,
Sarang, PPS, sports meet, anniversary,
GDs, quizzes, records, laboratory,
of 4 years, this is just a brief itinerary.

just a few days of college ahead,
yet it seems like there's lot unsaid,
unfelt, untold, unheard, unread,
wanting to go back in time instead.

now there's concern for attendance no more,
the canteen will be missed for sure,
there was someone in this place before,
and now someone'll replace us in this corridor.

it was chance by which we met each other,
in times of good n bad accompanied one another,
treasured all the moments that we spent together,
and it's a promise that will be in touch forever.

Not so close

There is a pounding of some sort
Echoing all across
She wonders what's the noise
As if coming from the void
Late night on this stroll
With a look little bizarre
She questions with blue eyes
Her little round sapphires
Shining under moon light
Letting out worried sighs
She grabs my arm tight
I assure it's alright
saying it's just us in the street
But don't come so close to me
You may hear my heartbeat!

You were there

Number of friends for me, never did I care,
Because I always thought, for me you were there.

My ideas views with none, and never did I share,
Because I always thought, for me you were there.

Never was I afraid, and many I did dare,
Because I always thought, even if I cry you will be there.

Never did I take a chance, to depress or to frustrate,
Because I always had a hope, that for me you would be
there.

Even when left alone, I always felt safe,
Because I strongly believed, for me wouldn't you be
there!?

But I felt my heart trembling, that something's going
unfair,
I ran to my heart, believing that you'll be there.

I ran only to find it broken, Felt I couldn't bear,
Came out to see who did this, among them you were
there!

Rejection

From the day she said we can't be together,
insecurity started to prevail,
in and around me; my soul
became a captive and my body its jail.

Though I am in my own house I feel deserted,
as if I lost everything; mind becomes unstable
abandoned by happiness forever
I feel helpless, tears become uncontrollable.

I am thrown away aimlessly into void,
I am falling & am unable to grip anything,
I know the sudden stop's gonna kill me
but this fall threatens more than the ending.

I leave everyone & everything and go far away,
but the feeling still haunts me
now something heavy & hollow lies inside,
where once my heart used to be.

I don't feel the sense of life, no purpose to drive,
if not with you, it doesn't matter anymore
how or how long I survive
life becomes fully meaningless for sure

Thought of you

The class was never interesting than this day,
coffee was never richer than how it is today,
I was never content with myself as I am now,
the song I am listening was never before so *impresso*
The whole day's a little special and new,
may be cause early in the morning I thought of you

Broken

The lights are fading, the picture is tearing
The colors are jaded and I wonder staring
Some things are falling in and some falling apart
I am sleeping tonight with a broken heart

A distinct sound seems resonating afar
Like chunks of glass shuffling in a jar
So close to a dark nightmare I see
But everyone is moving away from me

Carrying a rose tree in a city 'desert'ed
Counting the petals that slowly have been shed
roses start wilting and thorns over-bred
I weep holding a broken heart in my bed

A turbulent hurricane of familiar memories
Blows the castles of a good night's sweet dreams
Every single piece rushes to me like a dart
And sticks on my chest in the shape of broken heart

Lights continue to fade, eyes fill with tears
Everything blacks out with no concept of color
Consciousness leaves taking with it all thought
All I am left to sleep with is a broken heart

Pessimistic

The wind never whispered
The moon was always silent
I imagined a conversation
Whenever I became impatient

They were just simple dots, those stars
I was exaggerating the scene
I said they were forming your name
I wanted something for them to mean

In their poems and their songs
The different worlds they wrote about
I tried if I would experience them
But I saw nothing of that sort

If it doesn't feel special then it isn't true
That was how i concluded this
Pushed to the edge of desperation
I doubted if I was just pretending it

But sure, I couldn't sleep, felt unease
I could not focus on any task
Kept thinking when I would talk
What I should tell you and what to ask

Just a feeling of relief, no angst, no grief
When together that was how it seemed
Nothing unusual or extraordinary
Is how I would describe my love story is.

Genie, you are free!

Oh captain, my captain, why did you have to leave?
You showed us what a spark can do,
Why did you stop to breathe?

When you were battling from within
Did you forget about your cavalry?
You know you have inspired us
we looked up to you as your army!

You asked us to push the limits
Explore the soul and break boundaries
Yet you never showed a sign of your
Haunting grief or killing miseries

Oh captain, my captain
Why did you have to leave?
You showed us what a spark can do
Why did you stop to breathe?

Did you see us as strangers or careless ghouls?
Or parasites that would live on their hosts?
Or did you mistake us for those media folks?
Who would prey on your life for their shows and their
jokes?

Dint you know you could have given a sign
Why did you choose to fight it alone?
Immediately we would have been on your side
To rescue you from evil that took you from home

Oh captain, my captain
Why did you have to leave?
You showed us what a spark can do
Were you that desperate to be free?

Missing you

I sit silent beside the window
filling tears in my eyes,

thinking when you were with me
how every moment was nice,

with you by my side I never felt
the time passing away so soon,

sitting alone here makes me feel
every second cuts my heart with unseen wounds,

all I can see, can feel and say
is it's hard to be alone without you,

living in past, hating the present
I wish you come back, I am missing you

The one that got away

Never understood what personal meant
Until now, after all the time we spent
Smothered by silence in your absence
I couldn't approach anyone to talk
It was more of a private thought

Every moment makes me pause in my tracks
Slowly memories reel and turn into flashbacks
Intoxicated I smile, something breaks in me
I couldn't show where it hurt or for what
It was more from that private thought

Whenever I saw a couple walk hand in hand
Your face always flashed in my mind
The sensation of yours in mine
But I couldn't hold on to that part
It was all within my private thought

You are the only company when I am truly alone
Curse or a solace, I would never know
May be this is how it feels to share your soul
And they ask what is bothering my heart
I dismiss them remembering you are my private thought.

I keep coming back

It happens so that I am pulled towards the beach,
Whenever I come in reach of this city breeze.
Remembering those old days,
I wait for you at the same place.

In search of the days that we shared,
In search of the magic in the air.
Though you are gone, never to return,
Though I keep telling myself I am the reason.

A part of my past that I completely lost,
By an improper treason, to a peculiar cause.
A virtual reality draws me to this part,
Callous I stare in the eyes of my loss.

Memories of yesterday buried in sand,
Washed away to a distant land.
I keep coming back like tides of the sea,
To this place where once were you and me!

Way of Life

Decent Divide

As we walk along in these fields side by side,
I could not fail to notice a line between our lives.
A line that has been drawn to exist carefully,
I felt only just a trace of which initially.

As time passed, I realized how clear it was,
Though not rigid it created few of its own laws.
It was bent slightly by both of us,
Sometimes to my side and sometimes to yours.

But no matter how close I came to you,
I always had to remind myself the truth,
That there is a line dividing both of us,
There is a check on my feelings labeled as trust.

Now I confess it was nothing intentionally tried,
Before I realized the fact, I had stepped on to your side.
I pulled myself back the sooner I felt it,
But it takes time to dry the feet once they get wet.

"Time will teach everything" is what I would prefer
To say, instead of "time heals all wounds that we suffer"
As I won't call what you did to me as a wound,
Rather a song to which my life got tuned.

Yet this song wasn't meant to be in my album I guess,
The director just set my strings to play something else.
Now you have to know a part of me will soon be dead,
That, which has draped itself in your memories blood.

But this is not over, this is not the end,
I will always be there whenever you need a friend.
I appreciate you and that "you" includes everything,
Your worries, your choices, your love and way of living.

Acceptance

What should I reply,
When you ask me why
Am I awake staring at the sky,
Instead I would ask my life, why it brought this night!

Tonight, the darkest one in my life,
Tonight, I am scared to close my eyes,
Tonight, the last one with you by my side,
Tonight, the fact that you will be gone makes me cry.

As I look above and see the stars,
I feel like a victim behind bars,
With a torn blanket around my face,
I'm taken to a time where loneliness awaits.

Tomorrow I will be waking up alone,
Get ready and go to work on my own,
Your company that once was, will now be absent,
It will remind me of the times we have spent

The moments we shared can never repeat in our life,
We crossed a point worth remembering in this wild ride,
Though not content I settle with acceptance,
Because this is life and I believe sometimes *it happens*.

Enlightened at the crossroads

A little familiar, a little new
As I move ahead in this way with you
Have arrived at crossroads in my life
Which is giving me a sense of déjà vu
                    I have been in this path but
               It was with a different companion
               Now I am a little experienced and
               This is more interesting than it can
Was a horse riding with eye-blinds on
Looking only at the straight route
Now I feel like a bird spreading
My wings wide, looking at the truth
               I am starting to love this wind and
                  I am getting carried away
           Afraid if it would throw me in a desert
             Or take to a place I would stay
Wavering between flight and rest
Eager, afraid, anxious and unaware
A simple yes or no would relieve me
From this tension and feeling of despair
         Married to the wind, I would soar in the sky
           Hoping for a better tomorrow.
           or stop now and be taken as a pet
         I Would live and die without much sorrow
Irrespective of my destiny, though this
Freedom of flight is tempting
This phase of decision making
Is really smothering and aching

        I realized it to be a delusion at its best
       This freedom of flight and power to my voice
        I seek not this freedom but the one
      Which is a Deliverance from making a choice

For you

Tomorrow may not be same as today,
What all I feel, I may not be able to say,

One thing that you too would agree to,
Is that I haven't teased anyone as much as you

And one thing I am sure of is, whatever happens
The torture I put you through can't be forgotten

But somewhere in my heart I always feel,
There is little more acquaintance than what is seen

I don't wish to call this with a single name,
For I feel a picture will be confined if I put a frame

A simple message that I want to convey,
Thank you for making life funny all the way

Those Hands

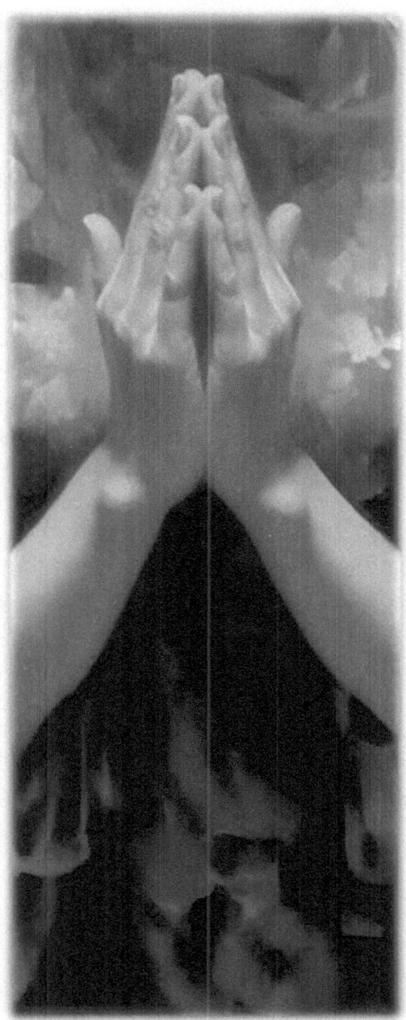

Whose hands
Are these
That I see

Joined as,
They are
A sign of peace

Abundance
Of purity
Held with ease

An entrance
An Invitation
A heaven's key

Enchanting
Made to
Slowly entice

Incanting
A foreign
Spell in disguise

obscure in tongue
but melodious
ready to please

a look at them
Seems enough
To set me free

Night

A mysterious maiden
that attracts me with its beauty
an object providing inspiration
making me blind, making me see

The time *when* light shines
on the path to my inner desire
the feelings and memories
in my heart, deep that reside

The place *where* I find
most of the ideas compelling
elating and enticing my mind
driving me wild until i am willing

The one *who* introduces me
to the hidden resident who speaks
the tongue of my heart I recognize instantly
to translate the thought, so that it permeates

The reason *why* I spend the day
and approach it for some peace
to put my head in its lap and lay
reminiscing the events as I fall asleep

Alec, you are the best!

Heartbroken and when you are down,
when your life seems to be a sad song,
when you wish he would come along,
lift you up, wipe your tears and take you in his arm

that's when you really need a friend,
a shoulder to cry, hand to hold, an ear to lend
that's what Alec did to her when she was left alone
he caught every piece of her heart that was blown

patiently heard her complaints & woes
gave her new hope with his soothing words,
he became fire that burned her grief, like a true friend
broadened her view of life made her tough like diamond

I wish I was your Alec whom you could, anytime, call up
who would be there for you at times of your break down
and break up
Alas! I was the first to become third person singular
but he was the one who made your happy moments
plural

I guess it was all meant to be this way, lest
how can I feel and say, Alec! you are the best.

Phantom Struggles

The days are gone, the people would have changed
They wouldn't know I am talking about which incident
But I carry within me the bag of those memories
That grows heavier every time I open it and see
I realize how it would have been for them, how I was
then
Soon I feel no point to dwell on, it's out of everyone's
hand
From where I picked this habit, I don't remember
Of making a book out of memories and surrender
My time, whenever I am alone and feel distant
Thinking I could rewrite some of it given a chance
But then I grieve on how cruel of 'time' it is
To destroy something that was once meant to be
Special to you, in deed, word and thought
And leave you with its memory crucified in your heart
It came to the point where I detest my own past
Every reminiscence leaves a bad feeling in my heart
I try to accept it for what it is, even though it seems hard
Like on the back of my conscience I carry a black mark
I cannot erase it, only cover it up at times
And knowing its presence bothers me but I
Remind myself that at this instant whatever I attained
Is the result of the same past and experiences I gained
I excuse myself of this exercise and unnecessary pain
Consoling with conclusion my brain can imagine
That maybe it's the human tendency
To attach a meaning to everything so we can perceive
And add a reason to our thoughts and beliefs
To justify our existence and have our say in these
Aspects of living, which for everyone are unique
we wouldn't want to be lost in a quagmire you see
No matter how you look at it life seems to remain a
mystery

For all the friends I miss

I was thinking of my old friends today,
wondering, from how many I have slipped away
I decide to call each one definitely this day,
but the moment I leave my desk, it is never the same
way
as soon as I return from work, weariness takes over
no matter how much I try, my eyes close and I start to
ponder,
I walk along the boulevard of my heart,
thinking about the present and my glorious past,
how everyone used to be just a shout away,
how I decided to rock today and die another day,
but now I die every moment and shout every way,
just to hear the echo dying & gone astray
In this path sometimes I feel,
broken dreams & fallen leaves is all I can see
wanting my friend to call me
silently wishing him a sorry,
for I couldn't call him as often,
and that doesn't mean I have forgotten,
it's like I am aware but am unable to identify,
the reason for my actions through which I can justify,
nevertheless, in this regard I feel no despair,
for it is never too late to confess that I care,
seasons change, the spring comes and new leaves
grow,
but I believe, a relation is never lost until we let it go,
things will settle and everything will be fine,
we are on the same road, our paths are intertwined.

Prayer

Forgive me father, for I have sinned
I looked at only those
That appealed to me most
Turning a blind eye towards
Who cared and considered me close

Forgive me father, for I have sinned
I listened to half of what I heard
Took in only the parts I loved
Thoughtlessly turning deaf to words
That urged me to try, to trust, to serve

Forgive me father, for I have sinned
I carried in me a bitter tongue
Filled with curses and sarcastic pun
Hardly grateful speaking the two words
Or talking of love or peace or fun

Forgive me father, for I have sinned
Betrayed the heart not just the one within
Misconstrued your words and the sayings
I realize all the wrong turns faltering forward
Appear and save me with your grace benign

Halloween Party

The crowd was good and the music alive,
Dancing with the crowd under the disco lights,
Boundaries blurring in the smoke, bodies in night
Screaming at the DJ enjoying with partner at side.

Wine in the hand expression going wild,
Feeling the ambience shouting with all might
Recollecting YOLO, to do what feels right
Enjoying the party, forgetting life's fight.

Distancing from the self, getting closer to the crowd,
Every gulp that goes in makes the music loud,
Under the possession a sense of freedom is found,
Mind goes into a trance and body follows as if bound.

Each with a mask, a costume, a different attire,
Judging others by using it as a decider,
None came in as their self in the room entire,
But we left the place dressed in our true desire.

Stranger

Looking into each other's eyes,
trying to decipher the stories they hide,
two weak souls in worn out attires,
victims of their own desires.

Tired and desperately wishing to be free,
a similar soul in a different body
in front when they see, this is what they feel
a rusted cog in a never stopping wheel

Coming across one another by chance
arresting each other by a casual glance
two strangers who sense a resemblance
in the life they spend in a social fence

Aloof from all acquaintance
finding solace in stranger's presence
the moment marks in each other's lives
an intense and uncanny assurance

You are not the only crop in this barren land
but a part of the generation trying to understand
their purpose, their goal, their final destination
in this impatient life searching for liberation

Belongs to me

Dropping from the sky in a single trip
Seeking a shelter as blissful as the heavens
The rain drop hits the leaf and slips
on to the flower making its grip intense

Reluctant to leave the flower,
Taking refuse and trying to remain
on its petals, adding to its beauty and vigor
Struggling not to be an orphan again

no matter how much persistent
The rain drop might turn out to be
It starts to get pushed instead
By forces that it cannot see
Acting as a shade from sunlight
Silently bearing the pain
The leaf that's no match to the wind
Bares the stampede of the rain

Trying to protect the flower
From the sudden and severe force
The leaf gathers all of its strength and
wages a battle with seeming foes

But as time passes the leaf starts to tremble
Hearing the whispers of the wind
Of how it might lose the fight
Because of the helplessness it's in

The tree keeps swaying around
Nonchalant of all these insecurities,
Hustles the water and leaves to the ground
As if declaring the flower belongs to me

You can't dance with me!

I don't know through what you have been
I don't know what your talent is
But you sure can't dance with me

I see people who could possible fit
Fill it physically & few with the soul for it
But they stay as strangers forever to me

You may never hear the same beat
You would never be able to follow my feat
We may never move to the same symphony

The music is different I create a different scene
Even if you learn it would be a chore or a routine
You would move soul-less like a zombie

So do not step on my floor, for you it's unknown
Hoping you can fill this gap to which I have grown
learning to flicker alone, who I'm searching for is me

I can dance with you!

Don't under-estimate my resolve or what I can achieve
You don't know the s tuations that I outgrew
You sure don't know what I have been through

I think you haven't known a girl's heart
If you are so ignorant of the things we do
We can bear anything we put our mind to

Give me love and look at what you receive
You will be overwhelmed , beyond your belief
I hold the power you are unaware of, you see

I am your muse, close your eyes, listen to the music
Forget everyone and stop acting like an amateur
Hold my hand , I am the partner you are looking for.

Four lines

With you

Holding light in hands, hugging the air,
Hearing the silence, feeling the stare,
Trying the impossible is my attempt to explain,
The feeling of being together with you again!

Not yours but mine

There is no way that you can escape my judgement,
bound to which I have my own imprisonment,
no matter what you accept or what you deny,
I will be judging you not by your past, but mine!

After few moments of silence

It's too
big a feeling to
say in words two
but it's true -
I miss you

Her Traces

She places her traces
everywhere as she leaves

Making everything
a minefield of memories

She believes

…that yes, it's all true
what is said in its every chapter,
but only thing that makes it a fairy tale
is *"they lived happily ever after"*

Tell you

How can I say how much I miss you?
I have nothing in my mind but you.
I sit near my bed lamp till night 1 & 2,
just to find words to tell how much I love you.

D&G

I would not call it a transformation arranged,
It just happened overnight I don't feel the same.
As if I have born again from the ashes you left me in,
A new day, new feeling, a new life I begin.
Only the name is same I am not the one you want,
You don't know me, the one you knew Is dead and gone.

Fallen Angels

Fallen angels with broken hearts,
Always in search of the other half,
To make us complete, so that we can reach,
The place from where we fell apart!